Pulse Points of a Woman's World

Pulse Points of a Woman's World

Sylvia LaVon Parsons-Ramsey

*Pulse Points
Of a
A Woman's World*

Dedication

*I write, even knowing
my words cannot last,
or think that the sands
of time would know
  I'd passed.*

*Yet, I can not claim
unintention to my crime,
my opulence of rhythm,
  my glut of rhyme.*

*As within these pages
  the words— need
  I say—I stand convicted*

*By my own doing,
  as soon you will see
  with your own eyes
  and witness my crime
  as you read.*

*To all who touched
  the pulse points
  Of my life
  With fragrances
  That linger still,
I dedicate this book.*

Copyright © 2004 by Sylvia LaVon Parsons-Ramsey
Library of Congress Number: 2010914374
ISBN: Soft cover 0-97277032-1

All rights reserved. No part of this book may be
reproduced or transmitted in any form or
by any means, electronic or mechanical,
including photocopying, recording, or by any
information storage and retrieval system,
without permission in writing from the
copyright owner.

ClipArt CDRom. "Art Mania 10,000",
Nova Development Corporation: 1996.

The following have previously been published:
"Mid-life" (Crisis of Lost Dreams)
    Amherst Society – accepted
    Emily Dickinson competition - Received Literary Award
    Published – December 1991 in *National Literary Anthology*.
"Alone" - Illiad Press Anthology – *Expressions*
    Published October, 1991.
"Reflections of My Mind" – National Literary Competition - Illiad Press,
    Published in Anthology, *Reflections*, Winter 1991.
"Armor for Survival" – Quill Books Anthology, *Down Peaceful Paths*
    Vol. XI – Winter 1991.
"Grey Days", *Broken Dreams Anthology*, Winter 1991.
"Missing You" – <u>Lucidity</u>, March 1992
"My Compulsive Urge" – *Lucidity*, December 1992
"Harlequin" – <u>Poetic Knight</u> – August, 1992, Featured Author
"The Hope Chest" – <u>Poetic Knight</u> – August, 1992
    <u>Potpourri</u> – April, 1993
"A Tired Vagabond" – *Potpourri* – 1992
"Dream Stalker" – <u>Dream International Quarterly</u> – 1992
"Dream World" - <u>Dream International Quarterly</u> – 1992
"Morning Fear" - <u>Dream International Quarterly</u> – 1992
"Bedtime Fear" - <u>Dream International Quarterly</u> – 1992
"Nightmares of an MRI - <u>Dream International Quarterly</u> – 1992
"MRI" – <u>Lucidity</u> - December, 1992
"Stranger" - <u>Lucidity</u> - December, 1992
"Sacrificial Metaphor" – <u>Jacobs Publishing</u>, 1994
"Somalia" – <u>Smoke and Mirrors</u>, 1994
    www.sylvialramsey.com

Pulse Points of a Woman's World

Contents

Theme Poem

    Pulse Points...15

Pulse Points of Youth

    Child-World..17
    Worlds Far-Away....................................19
    Memory Room Child.............................20
    Childhood Wonder.................................22
    Foggy Morning Magic............................23
    Bedtime Fear..24
    Dream World..25
    Morning Fear...26
    Growing Up..28
    The Hope Chest.......................................29

Pulse Points of Love

    Harlequin..33
    Love Again..34
    Blending..35
    Spring Magic..36
    Touching You...37
    My Sweet Repose...................................39
    Crystal Forest Fantasy.........................40
    Softly, You Entered My World............42
    You..43

Contents

Request For Love...45
A Rose For You..47
The Gift...49
I Loved You My Child.....................................51
Letter to My Eldest Son..................................53
A Dove's Lament..55

Pulse Points of Reality

Child – World Lost...59
Mid-Life (Crisis of Lost Dreams).....................60
I Feel Like an It..61
Dream Walker...63
Words...65
So Near, Yet, So Far......................................67
Dream Stalker..68
Grey Days..69
MRI...71
The Music Box—2..72
Stranger...73
Lonely—I...74
Limbo..76
Alone..77
Somalia..79
Reversal of Roles...81
Grief's Legacy..83
The Sacrificial Metaphor.................................84
The Silent Muse...85

Contents

Pulse Points of Wisdom

Memory Metamorphosis..........................89
Armor For Survival...............................91
Stone Lady..92
Winter Faces.......................................93
Grimm's Nightmare..............................95
A Mirror's Memory Record....................97
Little Boy Lost.....................................99
Little Boy Grown................................101
Mama's Crazy Quilt............................103
My Compulsive Urge...........................105
Serenity..107
Garden Paths....................................109
Reflections of My Mind.......................111
A Tired Vagabond..............................113

Theme Poem

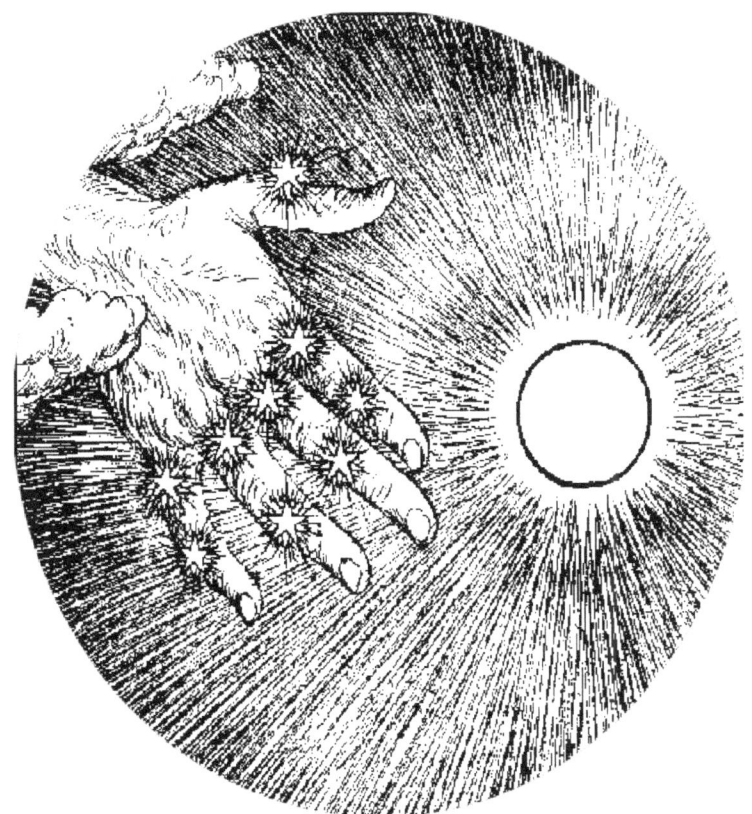

Pulse Points

Pulse Points

As the pulse points are caressed
 by life's lusty fragrant perfumes,
Treasures entwine the heart
 in the twilight of the memory room,
Where memories are imprisoned
 by the heart on an intricate chain,
Each link clasping a captive dream
 to be evoked to living vividness again.

There's a misty murky magic
 that creates a young girl's wistful dreams
Full of muted laughs, heart-felt sighs,
 and shimmering future schemes,
There's stardust fallen from youthful eyes
 onto a tear-stained crumpled page
That marks the day when a heart was broken,
 the day when Love came of age.

There's a grey subtle fragrance that touched
 the pulse points of middle years,
Where road maps were marked, "Detour here"
 for weeds of sorrow and furtive fears,
When the bright banners of innocent youth
 boasted Love's red roses and faith's clean blues
Were torn asunder and stripped of color
 by the odious fragrance of bitter truth.

Pulse points of the heart retain fragrances
 of memories that hurt and haunt,
That some how weather the wear of time to creep
 from the bars of the mind freed to taunt,
Bringing the return of what once was there
 held with a shred of faith and a hank of hope,
Embroideries carefully wrought with dainty touch
 as frail as thread and as strong as rope.

Pulse Points Of Youth

Child World

The childhood world of wondrous youth lives
   in an old frame house that laxly lolls,
Nestled among pines, beside a tiny brook,
   and in a remote community exceedingly small
Where a wide-eyed brat played with dolls
   that lay scattered upon the wooden floor,
While a silver-haired mother watched
   patiently, as she stood beside the door.

This child-world, full of boundless happiness,
   a world this child used to know,
Set in a simple scheme of yet another time
   was the wondrous world of long-ago,
But it lingers yet in the memory room
   though long since lost from view
And its every affluent hour heaps the heart
   with enchantments fresh and new.

In my memory room the child lives on
   with purity fair, haloed with grace
Full of pride and awe as her soft, fair hair's
   shimmering strands fall across her tiny face,
And in memory she lives enshrined in sanctity
   of home and love, not knowing as we know
The yearnings, aches, and stings of life,
   or the joy of woe that hurts us so.

World Far-Away

I remember, I remember a world far-away
    that existed on a warm, mellow countryside
Where laughing children chased butterflies across
    Red clover fields, rosy cheeked and wide eyed,
I remember a world filled with trundle beds,
    toy wagons wheels, bright spinning tops, Kites
Sailing on high, clowns in circus parades,
    juicy watermelon hearts, lemonade, and lollipops,

A world of spiral reds on barber poles, sticks
    of peppermint, gay glittering Christmas trees,
The healthy glow of a child's frost-nipped cheeks,
    wind chapped knuckles, ears and knees,
The warm glow of a pot-bellied stove, ice cream made
    of fresh fallen snow, soft pillows of down
In beds piled high with comforts and quilts,
    tucked safe in a world made of soft eider-down.

I remember luscious berries in a bowl of cream,
    sheets flapping on a line to a fiddler's tune,
Tomatoes sunning on the vine, the sweet smell of
    baking bread, homemade molasses on a spoon,
Preserving time for jars of jams and jellies
    to be stored in a musty cellar's gloom,
But of all the hundred memories crowding the list,
    is the one of momma on the porch with her broom.

Memory Room Child

The little girl who lives in memory room
    is apt at make-believe and when she sits to hear
Her Grandma talk, or read stories and tales
    of long ago, she does so with such a mindful ear
And memory for the subject and the words,
    that she will pick up a book and feign to read
Aloud the stories she has heard with such success
    that her elders are often fooled by the deed.

A pretty child with peach blooms on her cheeks that
    glow just below her hazy cloud of hair,
Enhancing strange green eyes beneath it there
    that gives her a dignified, "little lady" air
As she feigns the proper hostess and entertains
    her friends in the playhouse underneath the shade
Of a twisted redbud tree where hours of childish
    dreams and aspirations are tremulously made.

She is affectionate beyond the average child
    and of her few relatives she is extremely fond
Including the father and mother, as you know,
    there exists a strong loving everlasting bond.
So strong, that when her willful deeds of her impish
    nature cause her parents distress, she will wear
A spirit of remorse that will not let her rest for
    days, so deep will be her dejected despair.

The father is a blue-eyed, ruddy-skinned man
    who has known rigorous labor in rain and shine,
And the child sees him as a knight through eyes
    of awe because he is so loving, strong and fine
But even more like adoration, the child bears
    for the mother with her mild and plaintive face
Whose features, whether with a smile or saintly
    sad, is always luminous with fair haloed grace.

Youth's memory room is overflowing with a myriad
    of things that belong and live in another world
That no longer exist, but is secretly suspended
    in a simpler time, when life did not whirl
Around at such a frantic pace; but softly turned
    with an elegant grace that was fashioned of rich
Embroideries carefully wrought with dainty touch
    in each flounce and frill each tiny loving stitch.

Childhood Wonder

The wonder of childhood, found in the heart,
   is filled throughout the night and day
With the enchantment of a make-believe land,
   where magic creates a world of play
And mermaids splash in reach of little hands
   until the last little mermaid sleepyhead
Starts to yawn, needing a good night's sleep,
   so she puts the catfish out and goes to bed.

The wonder of childhood, found in the heart,
   is the wonder of dawns' recurrent miracle,
The delight of the smiling face in the moon
   that is set in a silvery white spherical,
Laughter overflowing, warm sunlight in rain,
   chambered seashells flowing with the tides,
Seeds of mystery growing and experiencing
   all the simple joys that life provides.

A Childhood Spring

A childhood's Spring is filled with spirals
    as gay as a truant rainbow split
With snowdrifts of gay colored confetti
    found only in a child's lullaby quilt
Made with love from a bit of silken cloth
    that has a misty opalescent glaze
Sprinkled with pink and white glowing petals
    filling the world with hues of April days.

A childhood's Spring is filled with scents
    of a perfumed pollen-yellow glow
As jonquils and daffodils blanket the earth
    when spring's first greetings show
Painting colors warm with outlines clear
    weaving an incense sweet and thin
To push away the lonely winter black and grays
    and let the warmth of Springtime in.

A childhood Spring is filled with silvers,
    delicate greens, and tiny fragile things
Like a lullaby quilt that safely snuggles
    a little sleepyhead that tightly clings
To wakeful hours as a young mother's voice
    softly lulls the wee one off to lullaby land
And she embroiders magical dream traceries
    of new life and love with careful hand.

Foggy Morning Magic

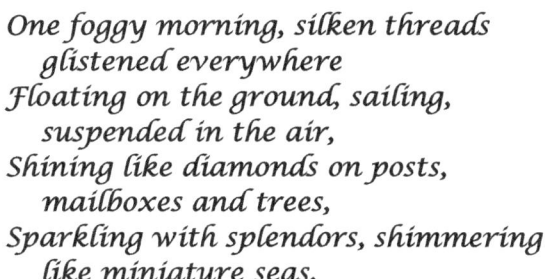

One foggy morning, silken threads
   glistened everywhere
Floating on the ground, sailing,
   suspended in the air,
Shining like diamonds on posts,
   mailboxes and trees,
Sparkling with splendors, shimmering
   like miniature seas.

It's a realm kept hidden,
   secret from you and from me,
Waiting, suspended in time,
   waiting in time so silently,
A kingdom of beauty, suspended in air,
   posing gracefully,
A kingdom whose stately Queen sits
   watching waiting purposely.

The weeping fog softly creeps,
   rolling slowly, silently, too,
A misty brume, blurring the images,
   blocking the view.
But as it creeps and stealthy crawls,
   through the morning air,
It leaves pieces and parts of itself,
   clinging everywhere.

Revealing sparkling, shimmering,
   gossamer castle walls,
A myriad of kingdoms of beauty,
   boldly to be seen by all.
But all too soon, the sun comes burning,
   bombarding through,
To deny revelation of these kingdoms
   from me and from you.

Bedtime Fear

Snuggled warm in bed
   on a cold winter's night
Trying to be big and brave
   going to sleep without the light,
While the silver moonbeams play
   with shadows in corners dark,
Where their magic creates monsters
   that breeds fear cold and stark.

Tucked snug and warm in bed
   behind strong locked doors,
Where the sound of feet
   on the old wooden floors
And the rattle of the wind
   makes the flesh crawl and creep
As the fantasy of a youngster's mind
   sees monsters in a clothing heap.

Clutching covers, the wide-eyed child
   finally cries out in frantic fear
Hoping her cry will not be in vain,
   praying someone will hopefully hear
And come to banish these fearful images
   that haunt this abysmal dark of night.
To give the door of the heart a shove
   and put the dourest thoughts to flight.

Dream World

The dream world is something hidden
   and remains hidden still
With its symbols beyond man
   and beyond his will,
Once there it eradicates the scale
   to judge his place and time
Where images brought to mind
   blend like sunbeam paradigm.

Worlds pass like ghostly images
   in a looking glass, melted away
Like silvery moonbeams haunting
   the early light of day,
Sometimes like a feather in flight
   mystically Floating by
Or falling, whirling, turning
   troubling the wary eye.

A world where all can be replaced,
   all desires have their certain door,
Where thoughts cannot express
   the foreboding feeling to explore
And when one awakens, the images
   have sighed and flown
Leaving mystical trees and dark degrees
   in the realm of a twilight zone.

Morning Fear

The morning comes
    with wind,
        and lightening.
The morning comes
    with sounds
        that are frightening.
But, just as suddenly
    out comes
        the sun.
And the frightening sounds
    are over
        and done.
The breeze is
    cool,
        and kind.
The fear was
    only in
        the mind.
The question is...
    what was,
        or is,
            the reality?
What was,
    or is,
        the fantasy?

Growing Up

"Dad, where do all the pieces fit
   in this puzzle that life has made,
Why do some pieces seem not to belong
   and why do I feel so afraid,
Where am I going, what will I do,
   and just who and what will I be,
These questions I ask and a hundred more
   but no one will answer me."

"Is growing up so hard a chore
   and must I, if I don't want to,
Can't I just stay in this safe warm world
   only doing what I want to do,
Will I choose the right roads
   as I travel through time,
And will you walk with me when
   the road gets too rough to climb?"

"Child, you ask hard questions
   with answers I cannot give,
For life's mystery is a puzzle solved
   only by time as you live,
I will walk beside you as long as I can
   but you must face this world unknown
And the time will come that you must
   walk life's road by yourself, all alone."

The Hope Chest

In a chest reserved for youthful dreams,
   a maiden planned her future schemes,
But time turned it in to a box of faded boards
   full of treasured loot and priceless hordes.

In the chest, shadows play hide-and–seek,
   and when it's opened forgotten memories leap,
Leap like hearth-flame onto souvenirs,
   carefully gleaned over the half-forgotten years.

That faded box holds dreams of yesterdays
   when a young girl lifted her puzzled gaze
To a far-off twinkling star in the sky,
   wondered about her future, then when and why.

Memory returns to a time when a wish was made,
   returns to follow time's twisting road that strayed,
Strayed like tangled thread in the sky's far rim
   to follow memories there, that years cannot dim.

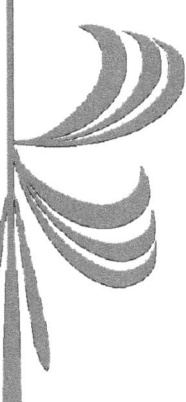

Harlequin

Upon our frail, unwary heart's stage
　the Harlequin called Love does leap,
Causing our sense of reason to be found
　only in the painted scene of sleep
Giving grateful respite, as midnight breaks,
　from our lingering, resounding fears
That the jester is playing at charades
　so he can laughingly mock our tears.

Whether Love's a saintly trickster,
　a Harlequin jester, or a fool divine,
Seducing the world with a frivolous nature,
　including this unwary heart of mine,
He creates a lyric land where life's a song,
　with love to the theme... notes are careless hours,
Where lovers are lost in time and space,
　pawns, in the jester's realms and bowers.

Love Again

We know that love is as old as sin
   and that is as old as man,
But with her wiles, she tricks the mind
   with her girlish grace again and again,
Flaunting and taunting with a dash of courtesan,
   hiding behind a new lift to her ancient face
Tempting weaving a spell to snare us in her web,
   to be sensuously entrapped in time and space.

We know that Love is as old as sin
   and that is as old as Time,
But we can't resist her wanton spells,
   siren guiles, her song of lilting rhyme,
Her wistful grace, wistful wiles,
   enticing smiles, and glowing youthful face
So we become entangled in her tempting web,
   to be sensuously entrapped in time and space.

   We know that Love is old as sin
      and that is as old as Love,
   But her charm puts our dourest thoughts to flight
      as it gives the door to our hearts a shove,
   For then she seems so sweet, her song so sincere,
      that her promises cause our mind to displace
   The wisdom gleaned from her siren songs before,
      so again we are entrapped in time and space.

Blending

Autumn's deep rich colors,
 and Spring's sweet song,
Mixing them together
 would probably be wrong.
Blended color and song,
 what beauty they would make,
But to put them together,
 what price would it take.

The essence of me
 is Autumn's richly
Multi-colored hue,
 and the sweet melodious
Song of Spring is
 the spirit of you.
Spring's song is just awakening,
 dreaming dreams so new,
And Autumn's fading glow
 is completely unaware of you.

Spring Magic

My mind and soul have been invaded
   by thoughts of you,
Feelings I thought were gone and dead,
   are suddenly alive and new!
Feelings that stalk and haunt me
   throughout the day and night,
Although I reject and fight them
   with all my will and might.

You are there in my mind with me
   in everything I do and see,
Even though it is only in my mind
   and not in this reality,
How long this Spring magic will last,
   I certainly cannot say,
Perhaps it will last forever,
   and maybe not another day.

If gone tomorrow, I won't wish
   it had never been,
Because the beauty of the feelings
   will cause my heart to mend,
For this magic is like a bud
   in sweet agony, trying to bloom,
And fate controls its precarious future
   which teeters on the edge of doom.

Touching You

I touched your soul
   and it was purple and new,
Mine had begun to fade
   to a washed out blue,
That touch sent my soul
   fluttering on high,
It soared with the winds,
   and touched the sky.

When back to the earth
   it floated, joyously down,
Reluctantly, so reluctantly,
   it touched the ground
And it was bright and glowing
   rainbow colors all around,
Soft and new, so fluffy
   like filmy gossamer down.

Transformed into reflections
   of a wondrous hue,
A blending of your soul
   and mine, purple and blue.
With your touch of purple,
   glowing it will stay,
Without it, it will diminish,
   recede,
      fading
         the other way.

Sweet Repose

Music interrupts my world of sleep
   and as I listen to the melody,
A figure, cloaked in darkened shroud
   enters my room and comes to me
To caress me throughout the night
   and then leaves me with the sunrise,
To wander hopelessly though the day
   yearning for the one I idolize.

I yearn for shades of darkness
   to hurry forth to bring the one
Whose touch fills me with such warmth
   it melts the shards of ice thereon
That threaten the essence of me
   warming, warming
       until desire flows
         tumbling
       like a crystal stream
       born of melted snow
      on a hidden
      mountain peak
        no longer frozen
        in solitude.

Crystal Forest Fantasy

Deep in the dark Crystal Forest
   the moon is high and white,
And as shadows leap across the sky
   to chase the chilling wind
A Sprite dances in an icy crystal ring.

She pirouettes with the wanton wind
   through the magical crystal leaves,
And atop the stony castle battlements
   spies a stranger watching her,
Mesmerizing her by his dark and piercing eyes.

The gentle sprite is urged to dance wild
   and naked for his impetuous seductive eyes
As though her spirit he would beguile
   like the wind that caressingly taunts her,
Provoking her to use seductive fairy magic
   to impart a fiery passionate summons.

The stranger's eyes that held her in their g[aze]
    now, fall prey to her wanton call
And the owner is coaxed from his dream sta[te],
    compelled to touch her fulgent flesh, desiring
Her to yield and disappear with him
    into the Crystal Forest mist as one.

Passion rises in this moment of solitude,
    the eyes coalesce in mental interplay,
Senses are awakened when physically, fingers roam,
    minds meld, if comparing the two, and search,
For the sprite and he are two who know that soon
    they'll know the sensual pleasures that wait.

Softly, You Entered My World

You softly entered my world
    filled with icy crystal leaves
That chilled the very soul of me,
    in the stillness of the night,
You so softly entered my world.

Softly, you entered my world,
    looked into my soul chilled
By wretched hollow loneliness
    that turned my world grey.
Softly, you explored my world.

You entered my world so softly
    carrying with you the magic key
That lit the world and lit a fire
    within the icy core of me
And softly you learn the essence of me.

You entered my world softly
    infusing my reality with embers of fire,
Freeing me from bonds seen by none,
    releasing my spirit to finally soar
Needing to escape my icy world with you.

You

When I am with you
    Space is limitless, and
        Time is without meaning.

When I am with you,
    Love explodes, into
        Flowers like music on
            Vibrating notes rising
                To a crescendo!

When I am with you,
    The highest heights
        Can be scaled,
            Fear is non-existent.

When I am with you,
    The farthest distances
        Even to galaxies unknown
            Are but stepping stones
                To ecstasy

We are lovers eternal,
    Who can be parted for only
        Brief moments in the
            River of time.

When I am with you,
    Is to love
        Is to live,
            Is to be.

Request Of Love

Beloved, only one thing of you I ask
  as we travel this road of love
And that boon I request is to carve
  my name upon your heart
So that while it beats with life
  I may live within you,
And should that heart cease to beat
   the love would be taken from my name
    Because my name
      would matter no longer,
        No more than a sandcastle
          the tide had washed away.

A Rose For You

I could send my Love a red rose
    for it is like a flacon
        that whispers of passion.

I could send my Love a white rose
    for it is like a dove
        that breathes of love.

But instead I'll send my love
    a cream-white rosebud
        with a flush on its petal-tips

Because it is the love
    that is purest and sweetest
        with a kiss of desire upon its lips.

The Gift
(Dedicated to my Father)

Brilliant reds, yellow, oranges, and greens,
The loveliest colors I have ever seen,
All cast against a bright radiant blue sky,
With snowy white clouds sailing way up high.

The air is icy crisp; the ground is snow white,
Because Jack Frost painted during the night,
Its beauty its grandeur is in sight all around,
It is like music, without any sound.

No matter where I go, what I see, or do,
The melody of fall will remind me of you,
To me, you gave all these things and more,
The ability to see, to know what life is for.

True happiness is here, it is all around,
In the simple things is where it is found,
And all these lovely gifts you gave to me,
Including the priceless ability to feel and see.

I Loved You My Child

I loved you my child...enough to say where
Are you going, with whom, who will be there,
To wait up for hours pacing, awaiting your return,
Feeling relief when you arrive, but acting stern.

I loved you my child... enough to let you see
All the parts of the person that make up me,
My feelings of anger, even those of disgust,
Including tears shed over betrayal of trust.

I loved you my child... enough to say "No"
And mean it, even when you hated me for it so,
Especially when you were half-grown and tall,
For me, that was the most painful part of all.

I loved you my child... and I still do,
I love all the things that make you, you,
I love you my child... and I always will
Throughout the hours, the days, the years, until...

Letter To My Eldest Son

*Son, I could not stand watching calmly aside
While you committed slow but certain suicide,
Waiting, awake at night fearing the unknown,
Sitting by myself in the dark, praying alone.*

*I worry that you are on streets of a strange town,
In a dark hallway, where no love can be found,
Captive of your need, surrounded by strange faces
Where cold, hunger, and fear stalks and paces.*

*Worse, I worry that your faith may be broken
And think that my love was only a fake token,
But my love was so it was breaking me in two,
I could not watch what you were doing to you.*

*Wherever you may be wandering in this land,
Son, I too pay the price for taking a stand,
I still love you and pray that you have found
Peace with yourself and are safe and sound.*

A Dove's Lament

Today I walked down the road of endless time,
Felt another's suffering as if it were mine,
Watched a tiny heart break wrenched with pain,
Felt the scourging of grief's agony over again.

I blenched and stared with a stricken gaze
While an eternity passed me by in a haze,
I turned and looked another way, but still she stood
Reaping this cruel reward, without mask or hood.

I never saw such loss or agony on any face,
And needless pain, I wanted to erase,
But life has no anesthesia for the searing pain
Of breaking hearts except what time can gain.

She stood like a statue beside her dead mate
In the middle of the road, awaiting her fate
Facing the oncoming cars without blinking an eye,
Standing bathed in torture, she waited to die.

For her time had stood still, life at its end
As death hovered above her ready to descend,
She stood frozen in time, immobilized by lost love,
As my heart reached out to a bird, aching for a dove.

I felt the anguish and tears began to flow
As I watched death's cruel hand take its blow.
"How silly," I said, "to feel empathy with a bird",
But I knew, not feeling would be the thing absurd.

Child-World Lost

Once there was a fairy land where all
   was always fair, fresh, and new,
Where has it gone...the Child-World,
   where youth's brave banners flew
As the wide-eyed child lifted his puzzled gaze
   to watch the drifting clouds in the sky,
While waiting patiently for time to move
   not rushing, pushing, wanting it to fly.

Once there were glad gay days and long
   young years full of brave dear schemes,
With splendid dreams full of rainbows
   fair and fresh, full of dreams,
Where the dark of reality's gloom
   was remote as a far—off winking star,
With no room for thoughts of pain or doom.

Where has it gone...the Child-World
   with its shimmering veils stripped, torn,
Where hopes, dreams have given way to furtive fears
   causing its shining armor to be scarred and worn,
Where stardust has fallen from youthful eyes
   leaving only stains of tears on a crumpled page,
With long melancholy silences afterwards
   because the Child-World has come of age.

Mid-life
(Crisis of Lost Dreams)

Hanging on,
    can't go up,
        can't go down.

Getting tired,
    giving up,
        hitting ground.

End the struggle,
    end the pain,
        nothing more to gain.

Fading, growing dim,
    a ghostly image,
        a might have been.

Flickering, can barely see,
    the flame, the image,
        that once was me.

I Feel Like an It

I feel like an It,
    Never a she,
Not even a buddy,
    That is a he.
I feel like an It,
    Working a job,
Cleaning a house,
    Feeding a mob.

An It, washing clothes,
    Paying the bills,
Wiping kids' noses,
    Nursing all ills.
A tiresome old It,
    Whose expected to give,
Making life pleasant,
    For others to live.

I feel like an It,
    Never a She,
No one knows there is
    A real me.
But It is a She,
    Needing others to share,
Giving her love,
    And showing they care.

Dream Walker

I am a lonely dream-walker,
  an isolated escape-stalker
In an age of not believing,
  but so craftily deceiving.

Escaping the frightful din
  this mechanical world is in,
Filled with people-like machines
  and cold money-making schemes.

So, I dream-walk trying to find
  a world more caring and kind,
Filled with treasures now so rare
  where people dream, love, and care.

Words

*Words can be like daggers
    that slash and cut the soul,
Leaving jagged cuts with unhealing
    scars that take their toll,
And they attain full measure
    of my excruciating pain,
Leaving me, a sacrifice,
    to be rendered again and again.*

*If your vindictive anger must slake
    its thirst in revenge insane,
Have mercy, spill my blood instead,
    so that my soul may live again.
Take a cold blade of steel,
    or a dagger, long and lean,
Make a sudden strike that kills,
    or a cut, sharp and clean.*

*Sharp, jagged words leave me
    with wounds that will not heal,
And though my heart protects
    the scar that will not seal,
Memory's ruthless fingers
    pluck the stitches from afar,
As slow drops of pain begin
    to bleed from the scar.*

So Near, Yet, So Far

Everyday you pass through my mind,
    my heart, my soul,
And everyday your image appears before my eyes
    taunting my path,
So, I catch myself walking to the chair
    by the phone,
Sitting down and as I prepare to dial your number
    my hand pauses,
Stopped in mid-air and I catch myself just in time
    to stop my action
Before I make an embarrassing blunder
    by calling you.
How can I so easily get lost in my need
    to hear your voice
How can I forget you belong more to someone else
    and not to me
That even former avenues of access to you
    are off-limits now,
Causing love to be a heartless, cruel passenger,
    taunting my path
As I wait, longing to hear my phone ring instead
    knowing it won't
A tear rolls carelessly down my cheek, as I ask,
    why does my heart need you so?

Dream-Stalker

Like a shrouded image
    in ebon black
        whirling, turning,
            troubling the eye,

The bird of darkness
    weaves mystic magic
        singing its song
            to the moonless sky

Spawning vile images
    indefinite,
        undefined,
            intertwined
                with its hidden

Symbols beyond man
    that beckon to us
        from its world
            baneful and forbidden.

Grey Days

I hate grey days...they revive life's harsh designs,
Revealing cruel patterns created over the years,
Drawing dark draperies of baneful dreams in lines,
Creating a craving for release from my ancient fears.

I hate grey days...when sorrowful memories pass
Like multi-colored leaves in an Autumn wind stirred
To transport pain in brilliant colors blurred
By time, like ash on embers or frosted opal glass.

I hate grey days...when weary hearts keep tryst
With one's half-forgotten loves that walk again
In grey-toned hues down garden paths hazed by rain
Where sorrows are veiled by the cold, grey mist.

MRI

You are placed, taped, secured,
   your head resting in a jailhouse helmet,
   tied to a coroners' slab,
   slid into a nether world
   encased in the arms
   of a sterile white coffin
   that is stark white, bright,
   and lonely as the grave.

At first, the sight and sound are white
   and sterile too, suddenly you become
   the only target in a video arcade
   trapped in a wind tunnel
   in the nether world of white
   as the weapons are aimed a
   and their continuous rounds
   of ammunition are fired,

And then, in the background a rhythm section
   of a rock band keeps its own arrhythmic beat
   while little elves with tiny jackhammers
   dissect minute microscopic slivers of the brain
   leaving you isolated, trapped, abandoned,
   in a nether world of white.

An emotionless voice announces your fate
   to be skewered and injected with cold liquid fire
   that later causes surging tidal waves of nausea
   that steadily ebb and flow like rolling, roaring,
   rumbles of Spring thunder storms
   in the nether world of stark, bright white.

The Music Box –2

Sitting there on a pedestal of clay,
   a sad little clown with nothing to say.
You with your sad, funny painted face,
   perched all alone in an isolated place.

Waiting for someone to come along,
   wanting to be loved, wanting to belong.
Your music plays when I turn the key,
   and you spin on your pedestal staring at me.

Behind that cold, smiling, painted face
   are pain filled eyes staring out into space
Revealing the pain and agony that exist
   in the broken heart that forgetfulness kissed.

Give voice to your sorrow and cry your pain
   for a numb heart's plaint as it prays in vain
And its fate, one does not want to know,
   s o taste the tears, let them hotly flow.

Stranger

There's a stranger in my house,
    I know not from where he came
But he wears my loved one's clothes
    an uses my loved one's name
While the rattle of his breathing
    keeps me awake with dread and regret
Making my flesh shiver and creep
    wishing for the one I can not forget.

There are night when I wish
    the memories of my mind were drawn
To block out the images I dread
    that dance 'til the break of dawn,
Wishing to see what once was there
    in the long ago gay days and youthful years,
Not viewed only through my memory's eye
    and blurred by a veil of wistful tears.

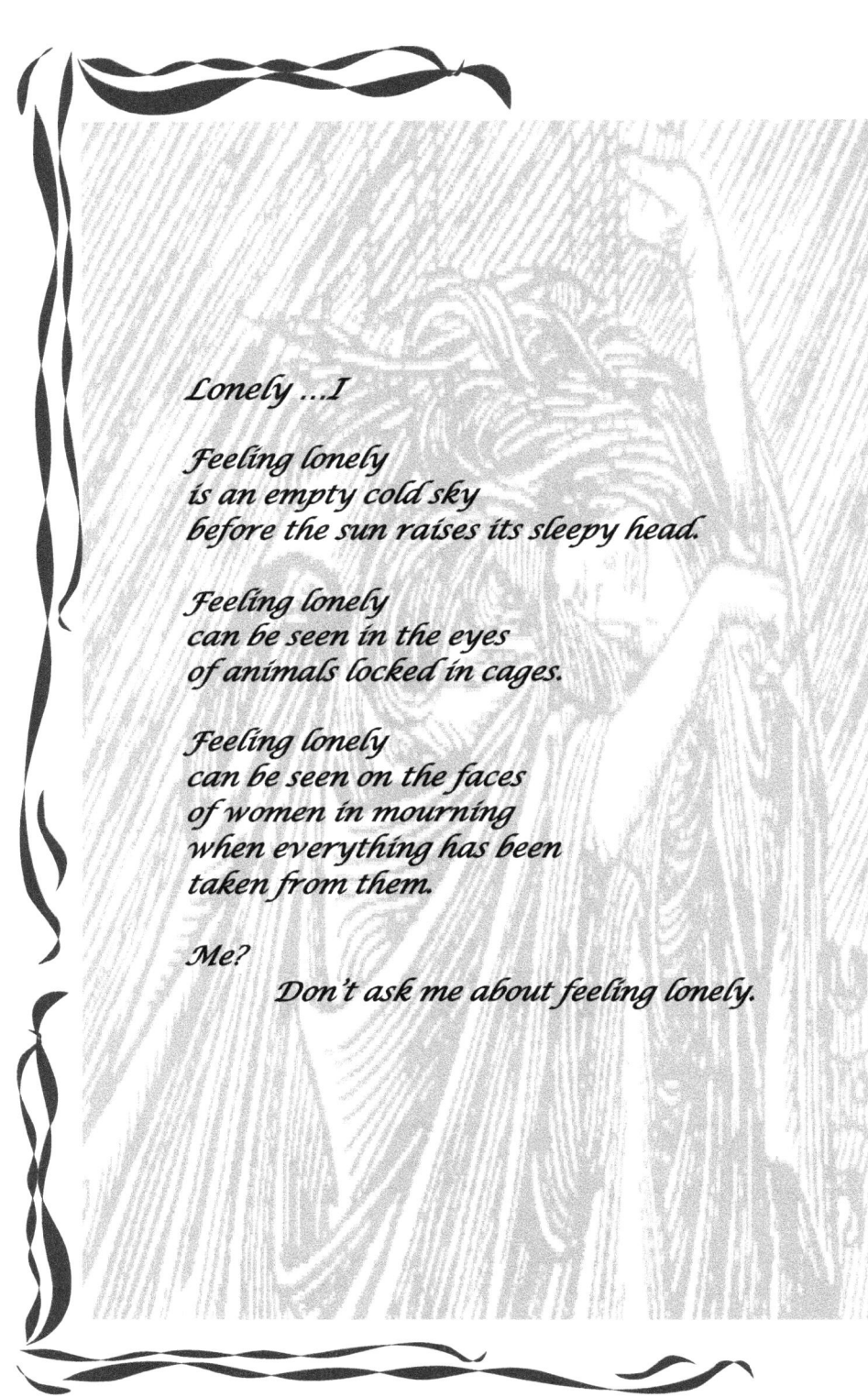

Lonely …I

*Feeling lonely
is an empty cold sky
before the sun raises its sleepy head.*

*Feeling lonely
can be seen in the eyes
of animals locked in cages.*

*Feeling lonely
can be seen on the faces
of women in mourning
when everything has been
taken from them.*

*Me?
        Don't ask me about feeling lonely.*

Feeling lonely
is a string of grey days
held together by rain
and a cold wind drumming
at the trees at night.

Feeling lonely
is the hour before sleep
that kills me every night
then pushes me away
from every kind of light.

Feeling lonely
is a cold hard lump
in the very core
of my being
that refuses to melt.

Lonely is me
    when that cold emptiness
        engulfs the soul of me.

            Alone.....I.....

                Not knowing why.

Limbo

Getting stuck in life, going nowhere,
    having no direction.
Being put on hold, not knowing how
    to make a correction,
Goals seem to have flown, like a bird
    with an empty nest,
Asking why, wondering, thinking maybe,
    it is just a test.

Life has suddenly come to an abrupt
    screeching halt.
Leaving you wondering, what has happened,
    asking whose fault,
Has the wrong road been taken and
    now you are lost,
Did you make a mistake, and if you did,
    is this what it cost?

Maybe you're sleeping, floating along,
    drifting in dreams,
Where nothing is real, a state of mind,
    not what it seems,
Will you suddenly awaken, released from sleep,
    and all will be clear,
Find you were merely musing, part of a fancy,
    with nothing to fear?

Your mind is filled with questions
    mainly asking, why,
But no one returns and answer, and so
    you faintly sigh,
Not knowing what to do, is this it,
    or is there more,
Won't someone answer me please,
    what is limbo for?

Alone

Alone,
    Me,
        Myself,
            I.

Alone,
    Underneath,
      A
        Lonely Sky.

Nowhere,
    Me,
        Nothing,
           I.

Alone,
Wondering,
    Asking why?

Somalia

(Dedicated to my son and the members of the 63rd. Signal Battalion.)

Grains of sand shift,
    slide, rustle and swirl
As the dust devil rears
    His evil head again,
And once more our sons
    are sent to a foreign land
Barren, harsh and cruel
    to even a tough, hardened man.

I see the war-pattern slowly woven
    by lofty, mortal men
Calling our patriots to watch
    and wait in the shifting sand,
Waiting to defy a man-made demon
    hurling across a stormy sky,
Waiting undaunted, to meet its fury
    aloft before it reaches land.

As I watch man create another page
    in History's war-torn book
I feel a fear that grows
    with an endless steady pace,
I know the agony, grief, and fear
    that only a mother knows
And I live a thousand lives
    in this wretched, fearful place.

I, too, live in a war-like state
    that a greedy man has wrought
In a desert storm, awaiting
    the thunder-devil's crash
As time creeps, and crawls
    at a turtle's wearisome pace,
Fearing my heart will be splintered
    by a demon's lightning flash.

Reversal of Roles

Roles of parent and child reverse somehow,
Somewhere in time...I face that reversal now
Becoming the parent's parent, no longer the child
Facing a harsh reality no longer sweet and mild.

Facing a fate woven into the threads of time again
And again causing youth to fade, wither, and wane
Making me realize how I have so carelessly strewn,
Wasted, time over the years, "My God, how, so soon!"

Too soon, I must take the reins of command,
But the captain of the ship, master of the land
Feeling a sadness in my heart that my time has come
But I have no choice what must, must be done.

I must bathe the once youthful body that bore me,
Feed the lips that kissed me goodnight so tenderly,
Comb the grey-hued hair once so pretty and brown,
And place covers over a lap once so warm and round.

Too soon I must face what awaits at destiny's door,
Walk the road of life alone, without you anymore,
Then the wheel of time will slowly turn once again
And I will be the one to fade, wither, and wane.

Grief's Legacy

Grief's legacy is treacherous
  like the flame-amber glints
In Circe's fatal stare
  illuminates life's harsh designs
Revealing the stark cruel
  patterns of the years
Dark and sinister, lit by tongues
  of flame that lick and sear
The tortured wounded soul
  cast upon an alien land.

Grief's legacy leaves
  a bitter metallic taste
Causing a dull nagging ache
  laced with twinges of sharp
Dagger-like stabs of pain
  as it slowly, methodically
Invades the traumatized mind
  like an insatiable flume of fire
To devour the ravaged heart
  and singe the tormented soul.

The Sacrificial Metaphor

Slice the page with sharpened quill,
    Cause tales of blood and magic
        To flow and fill the page.

Give life to bleeding ink
    Send its sorcery to stain and spoil
        The virgin, bone-white parchment;

Sacrifice the virgin papyrus,
    Cut and carve its fragile layers
        Reveal the fire locked inside.

Give birth to a living stone,
    Unveiling a diamond in the rough
        With icy heart made of stone.

Bathe the stone in living ink
    Polish it until it shines
        Watch it glitter clean and pure.

Caress its still, icy heart
    Until it beats and burns
        With inner fire and life within.

Transformed, virgin papyrus no more
    Metamorphosed by living ink
        Into a living, breathing soul.

The Silent Muse

Silence surrounds the muse
   like the murky veil
   on a smoke-stained rose
   that enfolds a city's dawn
   as the elegant words
   of pomp and circumstance
   are as voiceless
   as the cry of a city's neon lights.

In agony, he craves respite
   from the tyranny
   of a need
   that makes him a wanton, helpless pawn
   that lures him tauntingly
   like a siren lures a ship
   toward the hidden craggy rocks
   on cold, rainy, foggy, nights.

Thus, taunts this siren
   tricking the mind
   with ghostly strains
   of lilting rhyme
   to entice the muse,
   causing the need to be stirred
   when the mind's curtain is drawn
   to suffer silent, voiceless nights.

Pulse Points of Wisdom

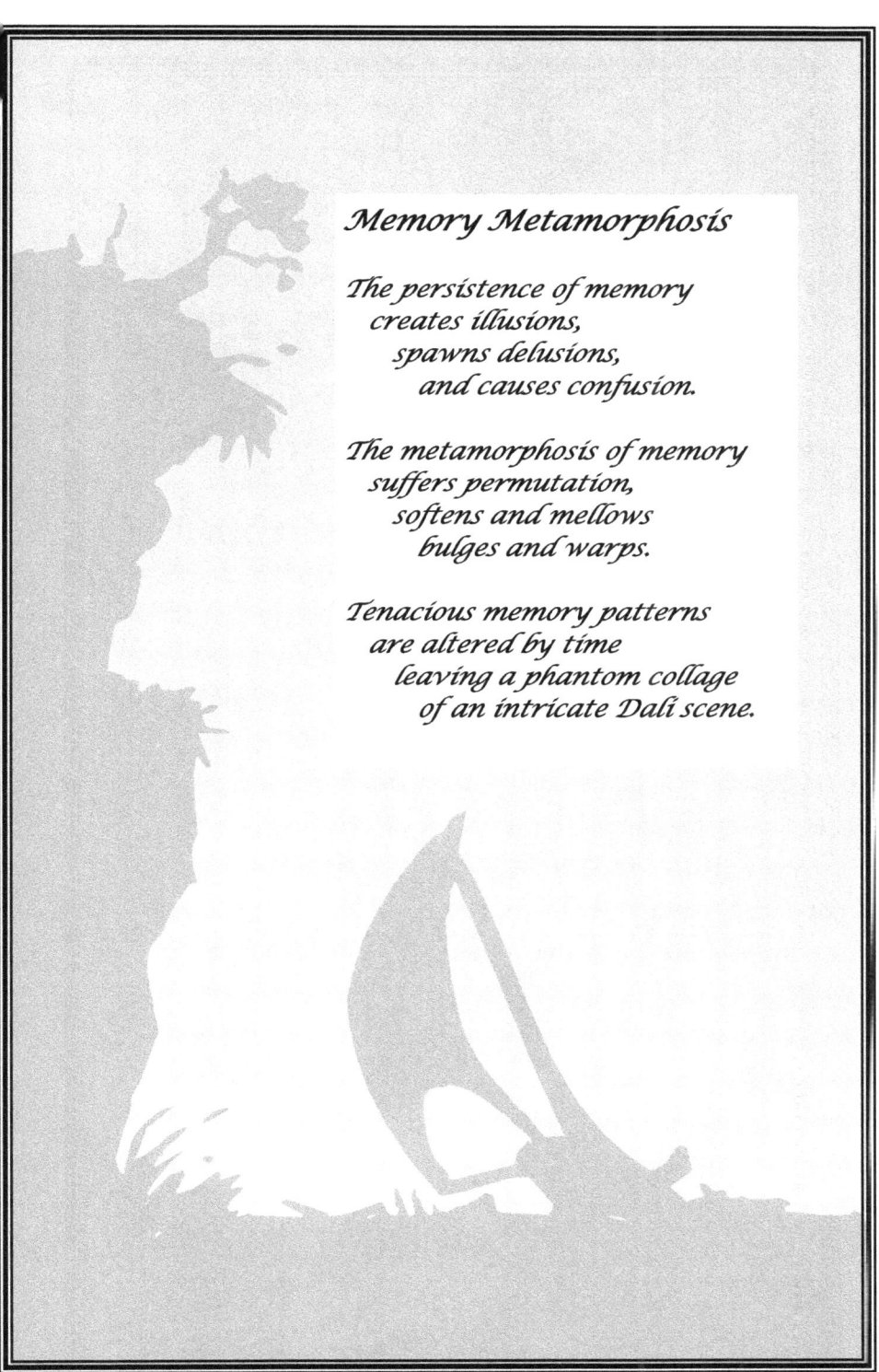

Memory Metamorphosis

The persistence of memory
  creates illusions,
    spawns delusions,
      and causes confusion.

The metamorphosis of memory
  suffers permutation,
    softens and mellows
      bulges and warps.

Tenacious memory patterns
  are altered by time
    leaving a phantom collage
      of an intricate Dali scene.

Armor for Survival

Let me love
    though love
        may go unrequited,
An empty heart
    is much heavier
        than a stone.
Let me have faith,
    though faith
        be often blighted,
Without it
    we are not
        strong enough
            to walk alone.

Let me laugh,
    even if it
        is bitter laughter
Mocking my own
    carefully kept
        secret sorrow..
Love,
    faith,
        and laughter...
Armed
    with these
        three gifts,
I need not fear
    tomorrow, nor, tomorrow.

Stone Lady

Face of stone,
feet of clay,
withstanding time
in your ominous way.

Eyes so blind,
they cannot see
what the ravages of time
have done to thee.

Oh, Lady with the vacant stare
open your mind,
your heart,
and care.

Shed the vines
that bind the mind,
and leave your cold existence
far behind.

Winter Faces

I saw the cold rain of winter
    fall like icicles dripping,
I heard rumbles of thunder
    bound across the sky, skipping
As I watched bleak December
    shroud the world in gray,
And listened to ghostly Spring
    murmuring sighs far away.

Like spirals of colored paper
    or rainbow hues in frosted opal glass,
I have watched the seasons cycle
    in splendid majesty quickly pass.
In each I lived with eager joy,
    and found my destined place
After many trails my restless feet
    sought to search and face.

A family of many hours, I found
    with a character of its own;
Spring is like a clear-eyed child,
    Summer a youth to woman-hood grown;
Fall passes with weary feet,
    a sad faced woman whose hair is gray
But who has tasted life sweet and sad
    and grown so wise along the way.

Winter is the woman no longer
    concerned with beauty or with age,
But faces the sorrows of living and dying
    like an ancient well-seasoned sage
Knowing to still the aching hearts
    that weep and cause wishful sighs,
She sings our sorrows and cares to sleep
    as we close the lids of our weary eyes.

Grimm's Nightmare

Passing like menacing phantoms
    three evil sisters walked this earth
Spawning off-spring that consumed
    all love, the happiness, and mirth.
Swiftly, contagious evil spread
    damnation, sad and desparate
Leaving men's hearts scarred and torn
    in a troubled hollowed state.

As Fear so cunningly seduced
    mankind into her wretched lair,
Hate used her wit and winsome wiles
    to capture and entrap him there
So Doubt could cast her evil spell,
    entwine him in her viscous web
Creating a world filled with slaves
    whose faith and hope began to ebb.

Life became a worthless symbol,
    a distraction, nothing more,
Filled with all the amoral things
    Godlier men used to abhor
Leaving behind ghostly images
    of men who lost a sinister bout
With the three baneful sisters
    known only as Fear, Hate, and Doubt.

A Mirror's Memory-Record

Staring solemnly in the mirror
    startled that all I can see
Is the image of my mother
    critically staring back at me
Like an older, wrinkled stranger
    with an ancient face,
No longer the sunny girl
    who lives a happy, carefree pace.

Where's the girl that looked so sweet
    in the gay warm spring light,
With a smile called cute
    and a laugh called bright,
And who's this one with wrinkles
    reflecting wrinkles of the mind
Gained by facing life head on,
    not running to leave it behind?

Who owns that mouth that smiles
    and strange face that taunts
With that look in her eyes
    that hurts and haunts
As the mirror reflects the loss
    of youth leaving a long dull pain,
Bringing to mind what once was there,
    gone forever, never to be again?

Little Boy Lost

Little boy lost with big brown eyes
    all alone in a crowd staring back at me
Reflecting memories clear and blurred
    watching, waiting for someone to see
The stains of heart-sick tears cause
    by illusion's shimmering veil torn
And stripped by neglect and pain leaving
    youth's shining armor scarred and worn.

There sits the little dark-haired boy,
    with sorrowful eyes that taunt,
Invading my sleep as they squeeze through
    the bars of my mind to roam and haunt
Like a twisted road that somehow strayed
    to leave me awake with mocking tears
Wondering how such harsh, callous wounds
    on innocence and youth can be made.

How can I reach this little boy lost
    with such bitter wisdom, so full of gall,
From forgotten worth by the wraith of life
    fighting a battle to survive it all, or ease
The suffering from many a remembered blow
    giving relief from the long dull pain
So that the bright brave banners of youth
    may fly unfurled and true again.

Little Boy Grown

The shadows of memory of my little boy grown
    play at hide-and-seek in the tumbled heap
Of things in a dusty corner of my mind
    that I do not know why I keep
Except that they won't go away, dissolve,
    fade, be hushed, or stilled
And, until the mind remembers no more
    they will remain, can't be killed.

There are pitter patter sounds of tiny feet
    running quickly across the floor,
The sudden knock, tiny pleas of a little boy
    begging entrance to my bedroom door,
There's a homemade kite, a green odd shaped stone,
    broken Christmas toys, strings and rocks,
A dog-eared book, a piece of crumbling fossil bone,
    a little boy's treasures in a battered box.

My memory holds captive a dream of a little boy
    who lived in a far-away golden age
Like a well-loved story in a child's book
    held captive in the heart's memory cage
Where memories are saved and years can't dim
    the image of this small boy's face
Filled with tears or smiles of brief sweet joy
    running across the field at too fast a pace.

Such precious things there held fast to keep,
    jammed full in every inch of space
From the topmost shelf to the crowded floor
    filled with treasures, aged with grace
A memory-record of a brave ardent youth
    with a smiling face smeared with grime
Now grown, a child no more, but a man
    who's boyhood lives only in memory-time.

Mamma's Crazy Quilt

In the cedar chest lives Mamma's crazy quilt
    stitched with love and memory thread
That was made by the dim lamp light as she sat
    and sewed for hours with the rest asleep in bed
Dreaming of Spring's first touch of sunny days,
    dreaming away the long winter night
While Mamma sat and sewed by only a tiny glow
    in shadows cast by the large phantom's light.

Its colors varied warm, bright, pale, and cool
    now softened like springtime images spilt,
Painted with age into a zigzag pattern
    that is a softer version of Mamma's crazy quilt
And I watched it change as time has flown
    to mark the days that come and pass
To now distinctly see that touch of silver grey
    and Mamma's face there in my looking-glass.

My Compulsive Urge

A great need arises and...I write
To capture great flaming words in flight
In my mind's eye I see and...I write
Bright words that flood my world with light.

I write...to emberize my hopes and deeds,
To feed my hungry heart for the beauty it needs,
I write...to bequeath the splendor and strife,
Voice my sorrow and cry my pain reaped from life.

Wanting to leave my footprints in the sands
Of time creates a compulsion and...I write
Even knowing that life's swift erasing hands
Will wash the silly prints away and still...I write.

I write, I write even knowing footprints cannot last
Or even think the sands would know I'd passed,
I write to quell the fierce driving discontent carved
In my heart...to feed that for which it is starved.

Serenity

Over the hill, cradled deep in the wood
A tiny, rustic cabin serenely stood,
Silhouetted against a blue-shadowed hill,
Reflected its warmth in a crystal rill.

There was a yard with trees and flowers
Where I built, grubbed, and toiled for hours
Knew the joy of belonging, felt the roots of me
Soothed and carefully bathed in sweet serenity.

Now as twilight years sprinkle in the night
My weary soul longs for serenity's respite,
Wishing to return to the blue-shadowed hill
And the cabin in the woods soft and still.

Garden Paths

Walking down the narrow garden path,
    as golden glints, and silvery gleams
Reflected in the dewdrops clinging, lingering
    like shimmering wistful dreams,
Taunt the heart like seedlings in spring
    promising rebirth of abandoned goals,
Stirring heart-felt hope and sighs
    bringing new life to tired, weary souls.

Down the narrow garden path you can find
    pomegranates wrought with ruddy gold
Powdered thick with stardust, showing hearts of
    humble grenadine, fashioned to unfold
Revealing an offering, a treasured bounty,
    of blood red garnets set as seeds
Among the leaves of carefully carved malachite
    where in the dark night a moon-moth feeds.

Walking down the narrow garden path
    when the world seems shrouded in gray
Lifts the gloom from the heavy heart
    to magic it away like moonlight in the day
As its fragrant perfume and glorious hue
    brings a casket full of jewels to hold,
Each piece a tiny fragment of the rainbow
    intertwined with sunbeams, wrapped in gold.

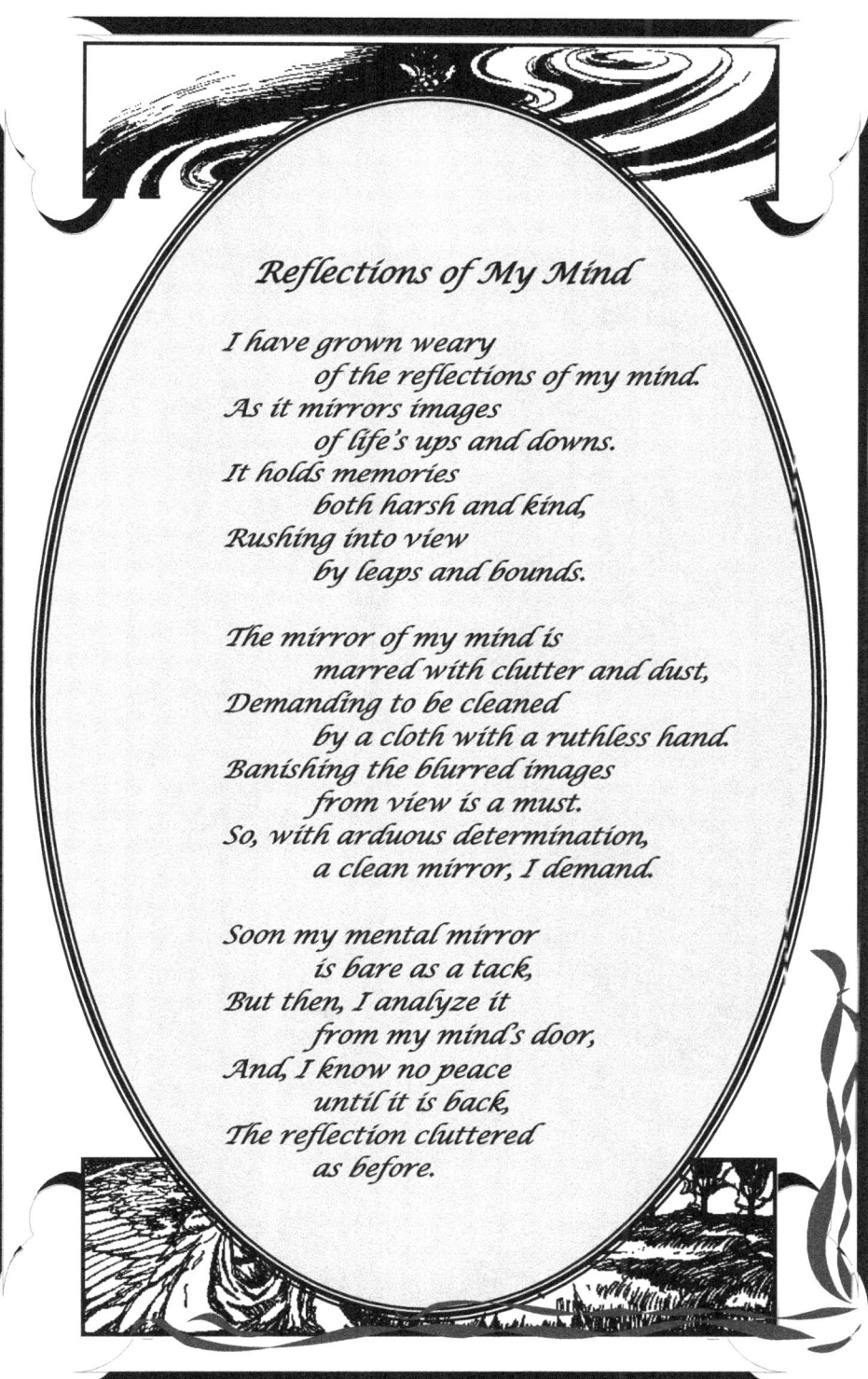

Reflections of My Mind

I have grown weary
    of the reflections of my mind.
As it mirrors images
    of life's ups and downs.
It holds memories
    both harsh and kind,
Rushing into view
    by leaps and bounds.

The mirror of my mind is
    marred with clutter and dust,
Demanding to be cleaned
    by a cloth with a ruthless hand.
Banishing the blurred images
    from view is a must.
So, with arduous determination,
    a clean mirror, I demand.

Soon my mental mirror
    is bare as a tack,
But then, I analyze it
    from my mind's door,
And, I know no peace
    until it is back,
The reflection cluttered
    as before.

A Tired Vagabond

When my feet grow too weary of walking
    through endless time and change,
When the wonder of life is gone
    and everything seems foreign or strange,
When I have played the sense-song through
    and wearied of its themes,
When I have lived life more vividly
    than all my maddest dreams,
Then I will gather all I love
    around my banquet board.
And when the songs have all been sung
    and all the wine has been poured,
When I have crashed my goblet on the floor
    and have watched the crimson seep,
Then through destiny's door will I slowly leave
    with reluctant silent feet.

About the Author

Writing has always been one of Sylvia's passions. She began writing news and feature articles for a small town newspaper in Southeast Missouri at the age of nine. Because of the nurturing and encouragement given to her by Bob Roberts, the news editor, she developed a love and a need to write.

By the time she was working on her graduate degree, several of her poems, short stories and feature articles had been published. Since that time over one hundred of her short stories and poems have found their way into literary magazines. She has been a featured poet in several literary journals over the years. Later her writing extended into the realm of research in the field of Human Communication and her work has been published in journals such as The Arkansas Speech Association Journal, and The Speech Teachers Association of Missouri Journal.

Her novel, An Underground Jewell is also available and the royalties she receives on this book is also given to the American Bladder Cancer Society.

She has experienced life at many levels. She is a survivor of bladder cancer and looks at the experience as another learning peak in life.

She is presently a Communications instructor and the Coordinator of the Academic Resource Center at GMC-Augusta, a two-year liberal arts college. She is also the Vice-President on the Board of Directors of the American Bladder Cancer Society. The main focus of the organization is to bring about awareness of an underserved cancer, give support to survivors and their caregivers and to provide sources of Information for those who need it. (www.bladdercancersupport.org).

When times are tough, she tries to remember some very wise words sent to her by a friend.

"When life gives you a 100 reasons to cry, show life that you have 1000 reasons to smile. Face your past without regret. Handle your present with confidence. Prepare for the future without fear. Keep the faith and drop the fear. Every minute of life is too precious too waste."

Her novel, An Underground Jewell is also available and the royalties she receives on this book is also given to the American Bladder Cancer Society.

www.ingramcontent.com/pod-product-compliance
Lightning Source LLC
Chambersburg PA
CBHW032139040426
42449CB00005B/324